DISCOVERING DOLPHINS AND WHALES

by Charis Mather

Minneapolis, Minnesota

Credits

All images are courtesy of Shutterstock.com, unless otherwise specified. With thanks to Getty Images, Thinkstock Photo, and iStockphoto. Recurring – Net Vector, Baskiabat, NotionPic, PCH.Vector, Latelier, Susann Guenther. Cover – Craig Lambert Photography, slowmotiongli, Willyam Bradberry. 2–3 – Vladimir Turkenich. 4–5 – Mvshop. 6–7 – Dai Mar Tamarack, Mike Bauer, Tory Kallman. 8–9 – Earth theater, Nico Faramaz. 10–11 – tee262, Visual Storyteller. 12–13 – IgorZh, RMMPPhotography. 14–15 – Tory Kallman, Vladimir Turkenich. 16–17 – Animalgraphy, lattesmile, Lei Zhu NZ. 18–19 – Martial Red, Ajit S N, National Marine Sanctuaries (https://commons.wikimedia.org/wiki/File:CINMS_Two_Blue_Whales_Aerial_Photo_(27877575362).jpg). 20–21 – Cata Hula, Subphoto.com. 22–23 – Nipun Saparamadu, Willyam Bradberry.

Bearport Publishing Company Product Development Team

Publisher: Jen Jenson; Director of Product Development: Spencer Brinker; Managing Editor: Allison Juda; Editor: Cole Nelson; Associate Editor: Naomi Reich; Associate Editor: Tiana Tran; Designer: Kim Jones; Designer: Kayla Eggert; Designer: Steve Scheluchin; Production Specialist: Owen Hamlin

Library of Congress Cataloging-in-Publication Data is available at www.loc.gov or upon request from the publisher.

ISBN: 979-8-89577-023-8 (hardcover)
ISBN: 979-8-89577-454-0 (paperback)
ISBN: 979-8-89577-140-2 (ebook)

© 2026 BookLife Publishing
This edition is published by arrangement with BookLife Publishing.

North American adaptations © 2026 Bearport Publishing Company. All rights reserved. No part of this publication may be reproduced in whole or in part, stored in any retrieval system, or transmitted in any form or by any means, electronic, mechanical, photocopying, recording, or otherwise, without written permission from the publisher. Bearport Publishing is a division of FlutterBee Education Group.

For more information, write to Bearport Publishing, 3500 American Blvd W, Suite 150, Bloomington, MN 55431.

CONTENTS

All Aboard! 4
For Your Information . . .6
Humpback Whales 8
Bryde's Whales. 10
Bottlenose Dolphins . . . 12
Killer Whales 14
Sperm Whales 16
Blue Whales 18
Spinner Dolphins 20
Back on Land! 22
Glossary 24
Index 24

ALL ABOARD!

Ahoy there! Welcome to See-Gulls Ocean Tours. We are about to set sail. Today, we are searching for wonderful whales and dazzling dolphins.

FOR YOUR INFORMATION

Although dolphins and whales may look like big fish, they are actually **mammals**! This means they need to come to the surface to breathe air.

When whales and dolphins sleep, half of their brains stay awake. This allows them to come to the surface to breathe.

HUMPBACK WHALES

That's quite a splash!

Humpback whales are great swimmers. In fact, they have one of the longest **migrations** of any mammal on Earth. Some humpbacks swim more than 10,000 miles (16,000 km) each year.

Humpbacks often leap out of the water. This is called breaching.

Humpbacks are famous for their very loud songs. Scientists believe these whales sing to **communicate** with others far away. Sometimes, a large group of humpbacks sing the same song together.

Some humpback whale songs can last for more than 30 minutes.

BRYDE'S WHALES

Bryde's (BROO-duz) whales live mostly in warm water. Because of this, they are sometimes called **tropical** whales. Many Bryde's whales stay in the same place all year, although some may migrate short distances.

Bryde's whales stay mostly within 50 feet (15 m) of the water's surface.

These tropical whales are filter feeders. They scoop up big mouthfuls of water filled with small ocean creatures. Then, they push the water out between their brushlike **baleen**. What's left behind is the food that the whales then swallow.

BALEEN

I wish I could swallow that much in one gulp.

BOTTLENOSE DOLPHINS

Bottlenose dolphins are very noisy. These animals whistle and squeak to communicate with one another. They also use loud clicking sounds to learn what is in the water around them. This is called echolocation.

They sure have a lot to say!

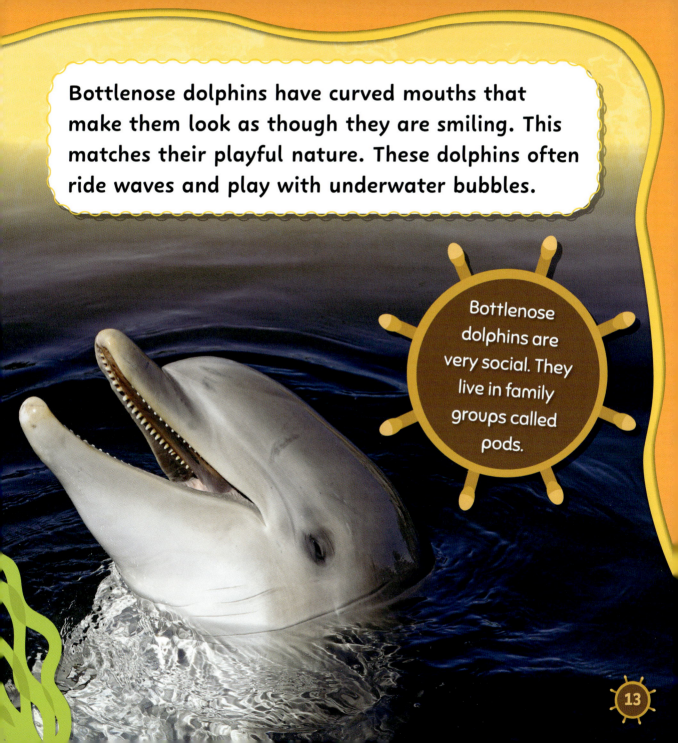

Bottlenose dolphins have curved mouths that make them look as though they are smiling. This matches their playful nature. These dolphins often ride waves and play with underwater bubbles.

Bottlenose dolphins are very social. They live in family groups called pods.

KILLER WHALES

Despite their name, killer whales are actually dolphins. They are the largest kind of dolphin, growing to be more than 30 ft. (9 m) long. That's almost the length of a school bus!

That's a killer jump!

Killer whales are also called orcas.

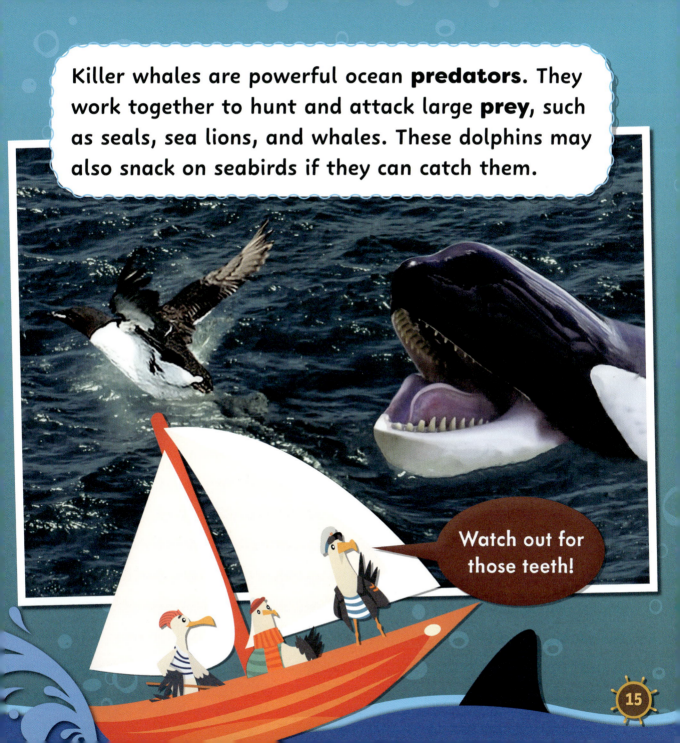

Killer whales are powerful ocean **predators**. They work together to hunt and attack large **prey**, such as seals, sea lions, and whales. These dolphins may also snack on seabirds if they can catch them.

Watch out for those teeth!

SPERM WHALES

Although most ocean mammals stay near the surface, sperm whales can dive about 10,000 ft. (3,000 m) under the water. They can hold their breath for up to 90 minutes while searching for squid to eat.

Before a deep dive, sperm whales spend about 10 minutes at the surface, taking in air.

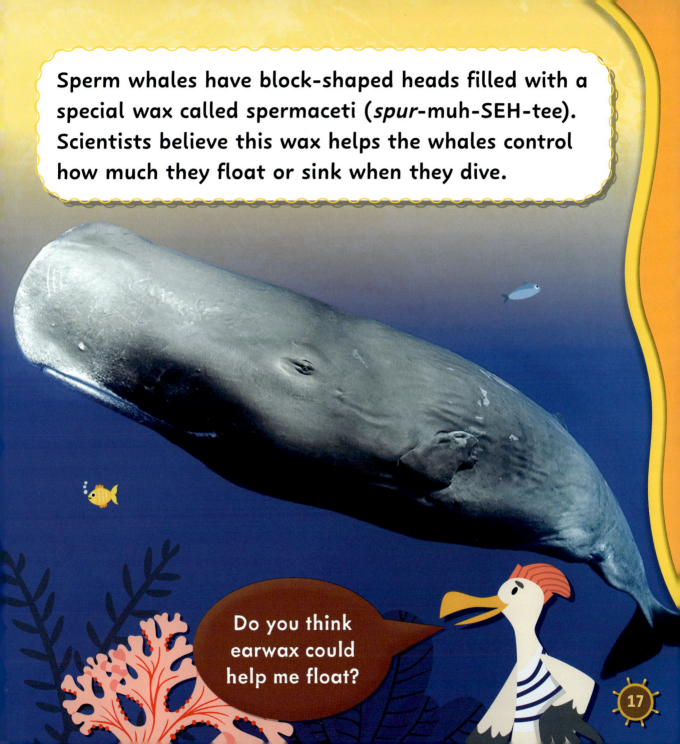

Sperm whales have block-shaped heads filled with a special wax called spermaceti (*spur*-muh-SEH-tee). Scientists believe this wax helps the whales control how much they float or sink when they dive.

Do you think earwax could help me float?

BLUE WHALES

Blue whales are some of the loudest animals on the planet. They sing songs that can travel up to 1,000 miles (1,600 km) away. However, they sing so low that humans cannot hear their songs.

Humans use special recorders called hydrophones (HI-druh-*fonez*) to hear blue whale songs.

Blue whales are the largest creatures on Earth. They can grow to be more than 100 ft. (30 m) long. They are heavy, too. A blue whale's tongue alone can weigh as much as an elephant!

Does anyone else feel really small?

SPINNER DOLPHINS

Wow, look at that jump!

Spinner dolphins are some of the ocean's most impressive jumpers. They can twist several times while in the air. These dolphins are named for their stunning spins.

Spinner dolphins can leap 10 ft. (3 m) out of the water.

Spinner dolphins live in groups that can have thousands of animals. Scientists think the animals may spin to communicate with others in their group.

BACK ON LAND!

It is time for our tour to come to an end. We hope you enjoyed learning about some of the whales and dolphins in the ocean!

Land, ho!

Glossary

baleen part of a whale's mouth used to filter food out of the water

communicate to share information with others

mammals animals that are warm-blooded and drink milk from their mothers as babies

migrations movement of animals from one area to another at different times of the year

predators animals that hunt and eat other animals

prey animals that are hunted and eaten by other animals

tropical having to do with the warm areas near the middle of Earth

Index

baleen 11
blowholes 7
breath 6–7, 16
communicate 9, 12, 21
fish 6, 11
float 17
leap 8, 20
pod 13
predator 15
song 9, 18